JAPAN
Activity Book

Author	Mary Jo Keller
Editor	Deneen Celecia
Assistant Editor	Linda Milliken
Illustrator	Barb Lorseyedi

D0474058

METRIC CONVERSION CHART
Refer to this chart when metric conversions are not found within the activity.

¼ tsp	=	1.25 ml	350° F	=	175° C
½ tsp	=	2.5 ml	375° F	=	190° C
1 tsp	=	5 ml	400° F	=	200° C
1 Tbsp	=	15 ml	425° F	=	220° C
¼ cup	=	60 ml	1 inch	=	2.54 cm
⅓ cup	=	75 ml	1 foot	=	30 cm
½ cup	=	120 ml	1 yard	=	91 cm
1 cup	=	240 ml	1 mile	=	1.6 km
			1 oz.	=	28 g
			1 lb.	=	.45 kg

EP048 • ©1994, 2003 Edupress, Inc.™ • P.O. Box 883 • Dana Point, CA 92629
www.edupressinc.com
ISBN 1-56472-048-9
Printed in USA

TABLE OF CONTENTS

Glossary

Bunrako—a form of Japanese puppet theater.

chanoyu—a Japanese tea ceremony.

fusama—movable paper partitions that are used to define and rearrange spaces inside a Japanese home.

futon—a thin mattress used by the Japanese for sleeping. It is usually rolled up and put away during the day and unrolled at night.

geta—shoes that are high wooden clogs with a thong that goes between the first two toes.

gori—flat wooden sandals with a thong that goes between the first two toes.

hago asobi—a game played by Japanese children that is similar to badminton.

haiku—a poem that consists of three non-rhyming lines. A true haiku contains only 17 syllables—five in the first line, seven in the second, and five in the third.

haniwa—clay sculptures made by the early Japanese. The sculptures are usually figures of animals, servants, and warriors.

hibachi—a small grill used by the Japanese for cooking.

ikebana—the Japanese art of flower arranging, in which the careful placement of flowers, stems, and leaves is meant to look like a flower growing in nature.

judo—a form of unarmed combat that involves throwing an opponent to pin him down.

kakemono—a decorative painted scroll made of silk or paper. It is usually decorated with a painted scene from nature.

kana—system of writing that evolved in Japan from kanji.

kanji—Chinese style of writing that was adopted by the Japanese. The Japanese written language is a combination of 19,000 kanji characters and 100 kana characters.

karate—a form of unarmed combat that involves striking an opponent with feet or hands.

kendo—a form of martial arts that involves fencing with bamboo swords.

kimono—robe-like garment worn by men and women in Japan.

mon—family crest used by the Japanese on clothing and decorative objects.

Nippon—the word that the Japanese use to name their country. It means "source of the sun."

Noh—a form of theater that is performed by dancers wearing elaborate masks and costumes.

origami—the Japanese art of paper folding, in which paper is folded to make animals, people, and other objects.

otedama—a game played by Japanese children in which three bean bag-like balls are juggled.

shoji—sliding screens made of wood and paper that are the inner walls of a Japanese house.

soroban—an abacus, or counting frame.

ukiyo-e hanga—Japanese woodblock prints depicting scenes from daily life.

taiko—a Japanese drum. It can vary in size from very small to very large, and is used to create many interesting sounds.

tatami—woven reed mat that is used for a floor covering in a Japanese home.

POPULATION

Historical Aid

Japan is an island country located on the Eastern edge of the Pacific Ocean. Four large islands and thousands of small ones make up Japan. Roughly the size of California, it is inhabited by about half the number of people that live in the entire United States!

Mountains and hills cover most of Japan making it a country of great beauty. These mountains take up so much land, however, that the great majority of people live on narrow plains across the coast.

Project

Participate in an activity that enables students to visualize the density of Japan's population.

Materials

• Basketball court

Directions

1. Ask all the students in your class to stand and spread out in a basketball court. Discuss the amount of space between them and how this concept applies to homes and apartments in their neighborhood.

2. Now have **all** the students stand in **one** of the basketball keys. Invite them to comment on the crowded "living conditions".

3. Discuss the adjustments the Japanese people have had to make in their lifestyles due to the dense population.

JAPANESE FLAG

Historical Aid

The Japanese call their country *Nippon* or *Nihon* which means "source of the sun." It is easy, then, to understand where the design for the Japanese flag came from! Adopted in 1854, the flag shows a red sun on a white background.

The Italian explorer Marco Polo heard about Japan when he visited China in the late 1200s AD. Although he probably never went to Japan, he gave the island the name *zipangu*. Scholars believe that the word Japan evolved from this Italian word.

Project

Make a Japanese flag to use as a classroom decoration, or a work folder cover.

Materials

- White construction paper
- Pencil
- Small paper plate or drawing compass
- Red crayons or markers

Directions

1. Draw a circle in the center of the white construction paper. Students may use a drawing compass to help them draw a perfect circle. A small paper plate also makes a good template for a circle.

2. Color the circle red.

HAIKU

Historical Aid

Haiku are simple and concise poems consisting of three non-rhyming lines. A true haiku poem has only seventeen syllables—five in the first line, seven in the second line and five in the third line.

Developed centuries ago, haiku remains popular in Japan today, with newspaper columns and entire magazines devoted to this art.

Over 300 years ago, a young man gave up being a samurai to write poetry. He became known as Basho, a master of haiku. *Basho* is the Japanese name for "the leaves that covered the hut where he liked to write".

Project

The most common subject of haiku is nature. Write a haiku based on a picture of the outdoors cut from a magazine.

Materials

• Magazines featuring scenes from nature

• Scissors

• Construction paper

• Glue

• Pen or pencil

Directions

1. Each student should choose a picture from a magazine and cut it out.

2. Glue the picture on construction paper.

3. Compose a haiku based on the chosen picture. Be sure that the haiku has only seventeen syllables—five in the first line, seven in the second line and five in the third line. Copy it under the picture on the construction paper.

4. Share the haiku with the class.

Haiku

The wintry wind blows
The blueness of its sharp breath
Chilling the earth's bones.

Oh! The full moon's light!
Round and round my pond I strolled
All the moon-bright night.

- Basho (1644-94)

SCULPTURE

Historical Aid

Some of the earliest Japanese sculptures are *haniwa*, which are clay figures of animals, servants, warriors, even everyday objects. These sculptures date from early 200 AD and were placed in the burial mounds of important Japanese people.

Beautiful sculptures were made from wood and bronze for Buddhist temples. The most famous bronze statue was cast during 1200 AD. It is called *Dai Butsu* (The Great Buddha), and can be seen today in the city of Kamakura.

Project

Make a haniwa, or clay figure of an animal.

Materials

• 4 cups (946.4 ml) all purpose flour

• 1 cup (236.6 ml) salt

• 1½ (354.9 ml) cups water

• Large bowl

• Baking sheet

• Toothpicks

• Tempera paint

• Paint brushes

• Pot holders

Directions

1. Mix the flour and salt together.

2. Slowly add water and mix well with hands. Knead dough for five minutes.

3. Sculpt into small figures. Add detail with a toothpick. Bake the figures on a baking sheet at 325°F (163°C) for 45 minutes or until dry.

4. When figures are cool, paint with tempera paint.

SCROLL

Historical Aid

A feature found in traditional Japanese homes is a *tokonoma* or raised nook in one wall of the main room. A decorative painted scroll called a *kakemono* is placed in the tokonoma along with a beautiful vase of flowers. The arrangement of the scroll and the flowers must harmonize with each other, the season of the year and the occasion.

The scroll may be made of silk or paper, beautifully painted with a scene from nature such as Mount Fuji. It unrolls vertically and is edged with a woven material.

Project

Paint a branch of cherry blossoms on a kakemono, decorative scroll.

Materials

- White construction paper
- Brown and pink tempera paint
- Drinking straws
- Sponges cut into small pieces
- Optional: glue and fabric scraps
- Scissors

Directions

1. Put two or three drops of brown tempera paint in the middle of a sheet of construction paper.

2. Gently blow on the paint through a straw to create a tree trunk and branches. Let paint dry.

3. Add the blossoms by dipping sponge pieces into pink tempera paint and stamping blossoms onto the branches.

4. Optional: Glue narrow strips of fabric to the edges of the scroll.

BROWN TEMPERA PAINT

WOODBLOCKS

Historical Aid

Ukiyo-e hanga are woodblock prints depicting scenes from Japanese daily life. *Ukiyo-e* means "pictures of the floating world" and refers to the changing nature of life. Actors, aristocrats, samurai and everyday people going about their business are typical subjects. The woodblock prints themselves are called *hanga*.

These prints were first done in black and white during the 17th century AD. At their peak of popularity in the mid 19th century AD as many as 20 or 30 separate blocks were used to color a single print!

Project

Create a woodblock print (*hanga*) using a foam tray in place of wood.

Materials

- Foam meat tray
- Pencil
- Plastic forks
- Tempera paint
- Paint brush
- Paper

Directions

1. Cut the sides off the meat tray.

2. Use a pencil to lightly trace the design on the foam tray.

3. A plastic fork makes a good tool for carving the final design into the foam. Use the tines to etch fine lines and the handle for large areas. Experiment with different techniques. Remember, the design will print in reverse like a negative!

4. Brush tempera paint lightly over the foam tray. Use black paint or a mix of fall colors.

5. Press the tray onto paper to make a print. Be careful not to slide the foam as you lift it.

ORIGAMI

Historical Aid

The Japanese word for paper folding is *origami*. When origami originated about 1,000 years ago, it was used to create intricate paper dolls, packaging and *noshis* or ceremonial tokens.

There is a Japanese legend that if one can fold 1,000 paper cranes, their most special wish will be granted.

Project

Fold an origami crane! This is a simple pattern, easy enough for beginners. Create a classroom decoration with a garland of cranes taped together.

Materials

• Origami paper or wrapping paper in 6" (15.24 cm) squares

Directions

Follow the paper folding directions on the following page to make an origami crane.

Origami Crane

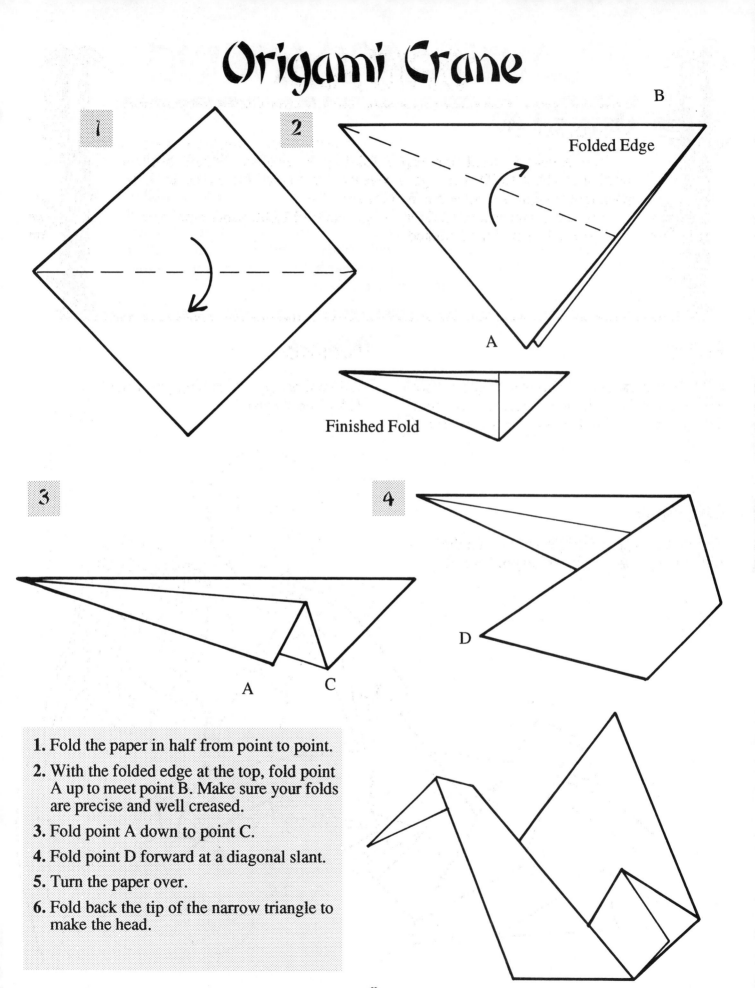

1. Fold the paper in half from point to point.
2. With the folded edge at the top, fold point A up to meet point B. Make sure your folds are precise and well creased.
3. Fold point A down to point C.
4. Fold point D forward at a diagonal slant.
5. Turn the paper over.
6. Fold back the tip of the narrow triangle to make the head.

FLOWER ARRANGING

Historical Aid

The Japanese art of flower arranging dates back nearly 1,500 years when Buddhist monks began making floral arrangements for their temples. This careful placement of blossoms, leaves and stems is called *ikebana*. Rather than bunching flowers together, each spray is carefully placed to look as if it were growing outdoors. An irregular triangle is often formed from flowers of different heights. The tallest flower stands for heaven, the next tallest stands for man and the shortest stands for earth. Extra flowers representing mountains, meadows and helpers are set within this triangle.

Project

Make an arrangement of chrysanthemums, Japan's national flower.

Materials

- White, green, yellow and blue construction paper
- Scissors
- Glue
- Crayons

Directions

1. Copy patterns on the following page and cut one vase shape, three flower shapes and as many leaf shapes as you wish.

2. Glue the vase to the bottom of another piece of construction paper. Arrange the flowers and leaves, drawing in the stems with crayon. Try to make an irregular triangular shape with the flowers.

3. Glue flowers and leaves in place.

Flower Arranging Patterns

LACQUERWORK

Historical Aid

Since the 5th century AD, lacquer has been used in Japan on items as diverse as hair combs and religious temples! During the 8th century AD, the government even gave each family a piece of land reserved for growing lacquer trees. Lacquer is actually the sap of the *urushi-no-ki* tree.

Lacquerwork is a highly skilled craft. There are many steps in the careful preparation of the item to be lacquered as well as in the process itself. A skilled artist applies many layers of lacquer to achieve a beautiful sheen.

Project

Make a lacquerwork box using the découpage method which is an ancient Japanese folk art.

Directions

1. Paint the box a solid color choosing from black, gold, red or green. Let dry.

2. Cut out pictures from magazines to fit on the box.

3. Glue the magazine cutouts onto the box. Let dry.

4. Go outdoors to spray the box with a coat of clear lacquer. Wear a protective face mask while spraying lacquer.

Materials

- Cardboard jewelry box (A long, narrow necklace box makes a perfect box in which to keep chopsticks—just as the Japanese do!)

- Black, gold, red or green acrylic paint

- Optional: protective face mask

- Clear spray lacquer

- Scissors

- Magazines

- Glue

FAMILY CREST

Historical Aid

In Japan, a family crest is called a *mon*. Respect for one's ancestors and family history is very important to Japanese families. Some family crests date back to the 8th century AD!

More than 3,000 crests are in use today. Most of the designs are nature oriented and circular in shape. A family might display their crest on furniture, mirror boxes, combs and even their cups and plates. On special occasions, Japanese men and women wear formal black *kimonos* that have miniature crests in white on the back, front and sleeves. A chrysanthemum was the inspiration for the Imperial Family's *mon*.

Project

Design and create your own family crest using white on black as on the ceremonial kimono.

Materials

- White paper
- Black construction paper
- Pencil
- Scissors
- Glue
- Black marker

Directions

1. Ask the students to decide on a family favorite bird, tree, flower, butterfly, etc.

2. Draw a large circle on the white paper.

3. Design the crest using the circle as a guide. Japanese *mon* are very stylized, so encourage the students to think of a symbol to represent their idea rather than an actual representation.

4. Cut out the design and mount on black paper. A black marker can be used for detailed parts of the design.

LANGUAGE

Historical Aid

Japanese is the official language of Japan. There are many local dialects that differ greatly in pronunciation. Fortunately, most people understand the Tokyo dialect because it is the dialect that is spoken on radio and television.

Spoken Japanese has different styles according to the situation. There is one style for everyday use and one for company. There is another style for speechmaking and yet another for speaking to elders!

Project

Learn to say a few simple Japanese phrases.

Materials

- Butcher paper
- Marking pen

Directions

1. Print the phrases and their pronunciation on pieces of butcher paper and post on the walls around the room.

2. Practice saying the phrases with your class.

English	Japanese	Pronunciation
Hello.	Konnichi wa	Cone knee che wah
Thank you.	Arigatoh Gozaimasu	Arigahtaw gozighmass
My name is Amy.	Amy to moshimasu	Amy toh mow she mass
Yes, please.	O-negai shimasu	Oh-nehguy shemass
Good bye.	Sayonara	Sah yoh nah rah
See you tomorrow.	Mata ashista	Mahtah ahshtah
For what I'm about to receive …(What to say before you eat)	Itadakimasu	Eetahdahkeymass

ABACUS

Historical Aid

A visitor to the rural areas of Japan may be surprised to see some of the shopkeepers totaling their bills on an abacus, or *soroban*. Although the soroban is no longer used in Japanese cities, older people in the country still use the counting frame. There are still schools where the use of the soroban is taught.

The soroban consists of a rectangular wooden frame with rows of metal rods that have balls threaded on them. With a little practice, it is possible to add and subtract even large numbers quickly and easily.

Project

Make a simple abacus (counter) and learn to add and subtract in Japanese.

Materials

- Shoe box lid
- String
- 50 pony beads
- Scissors
- Number chart

Directions

1. Cut string into five lengths, 18" (45.72 cm) each.

2. String ten beads onto each length of string.

3. Using scissors, cut five slits along both of the long edges of the box lid.

4. Push the string of beads into the slits and tie a knot snugly on each side. Trim extra string.

5. Practice your addition and subtraction. Say the answers in Japanese.

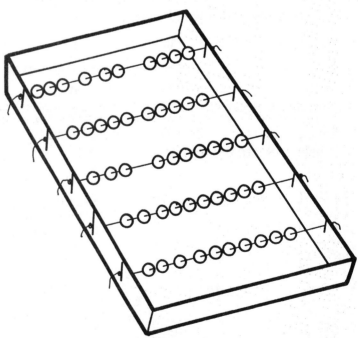

Number Chart

zero	zero	(ze-ro)
one	ichi	(e-che)
two	ni	(ne)
three	san	(san)
four	shi	(she)
five	go	(go)
six	roku	(ro-koo)
seven	shichi	(she-che)
eight	hachi	(ha-che)
nine	ku	(koo)
ten	ju	(joo)

eleven equals ten plus one (ju-ichi)
twelve equals ten plus two (ju-ni)
twenty equals two tens (niju)
twenty-one equals two tens plus one
   (niju-ichi)

SCRIPT

Historical Aid

Centuries ago, the Japanese adopted the Chinese style of writing called *kanji*. Over time, a system of writing called *kana* evolved. Japanese is written in a combination of kana and kanji. School children in Japan learn the 100 kana characters and some 1,945 kanji characters as well!

Japanese writing is a highly skilled art. Calligraphers, people who specialize in decorative handwriting, use a brush so they can make heavy and light lines.

Project

Write a story in English and kanji.

Materials

- Paper
- Black marking pens

Directions

1. Reproduce copies of the kanji characters on the following page for the students to refer to.

2. Practice writing the characters as a class.

3. With the paper turned lengthwise, have students write a simple story using a combination of kanji and English.

4. Have students trade their story with a friend to translate. Share the translations.

I WENT 上
THE 山
AND
見 THE
少 木

人	山	家
Person	Mountain	Home
日	下	月
Day	Down	Moon
小	森	土
Small	Forest	Earth
木	川	手
Tree	River	Hand
上	見	目
Up	Saw	Eye

BOOKBINDING

Historical Aid

The traditional method of Japanese bookbinding dates back hundreds of years. Unlike modern methods of bookbinding that use glue to adhere the pages to the binding, this ancient art involves sewing the pages together. Since there is no glue to dry out and crack with age, ancient Japanese manuscripts are still readable today!

Project

Make your own book bound in the traditional Japanese way.

Directions

Follow the directions on the following page to construct a traditional Japanese book.

Materials

- Construction paper
- White or colored paper
- Paper clips
- Hole puncher
- Pencil
- Ruler
- Yarn or embroidery floss
- Blunt, large eyed needle

Japanese Bookbinding

1. Fold four (or more) pieces of paper in half widthwise. Do the same to one sheet of construction paper.

2. Slip the folded paper inside the construction paper cover securing your book with a few paper clips along the open edges.

3. Lightly trace a line ½" (1.27 cm) from the folded edge. Measure and mark a row of dots 1" (2.54 cm) apart along this line. Punch the holes for sewing at the dots.

4. Cut a length of yarn or embroidery floss about 24" (60.96 cm) long. Thread the needle, but don't knot the end. Leave one end of the yarn longer than the other.

5. Starting at one end of the book and leaving a loose end of at least a few inches, begin sewing the book together by coming up through the first hole, down through the second, up through the third and so on.

6. When you reach the last hole, sew around the edge of the book. Insert the needle back into the same hole, looping the yarn around the spine this time.

7. Work back down the spine, sew through each hole two times—once to complete the running stitches and the second time to loop the yarn around the spine.

8. Remove the needle and paper clips, and tie the two loose strings together.

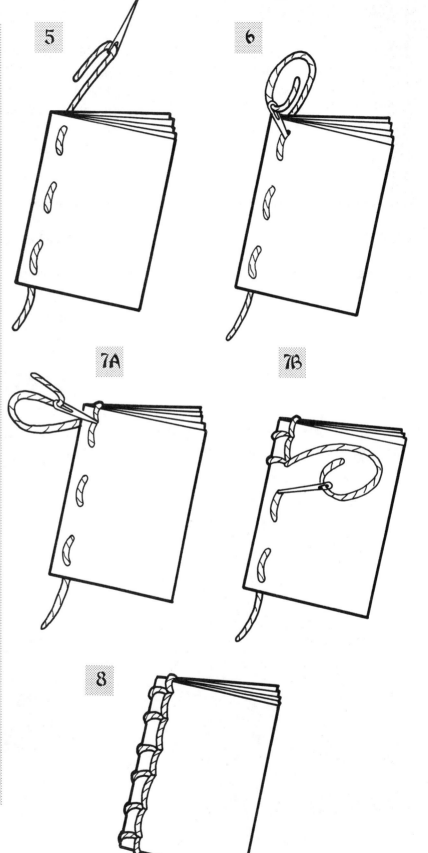

STRAW MAT

Historical Aid

In Japan, a woven reed mat is called a *tatami*. These mats usually measure 3 X 6 feet (1 X 2 meters) and are used as floor coverings. Most Japanese homes have at least one tatami room which serves many purposes. During the day it is used as a living area furnished only with a low table in the center and cushions to sit upon. At night it can become a bedroom by rolling out a light, thin mattress called a *futon*.

Project

Weave paper strips to make a tatami, or woven reed mat.

Directions

1. Cut one piece of paper into strips 1 X 14 inches (2.54 X 35.56 cm).

2. Fold the second sheet in half. Beginning at the fold, cut strips to about 1" (2.54 cm) from the open edge. Open the paper and lay flat.

3. Weave the 1" (2.54 cm) strips through the slits in the paper, keeping the strips close together.

4. Glue or tape down the ends of the strips.

Materials

• Two pieces brown butcher paper, each 25 X 14 inches (63.5 X 35.56 cm).

• Glue or tape

• Scissors

SCREENS

Historical Aid

A traditional Japanese home is a simple wooden building that is slightly raised above the ground. It is surrounded by a verandah that may be closed by means of sliding wooden screens.

Most traditional homes are small. To make the most out of the limited space, the rooms are separated by movable paper partitions called *fusama* that can be rearranged to change the size or shape of the room. The inner wall, or *shoji*, is made of sliding screens of wood and translucent paper. When all the screens are open, the gardens can be seen from every room.

Project

Make a small version of a shoji, or paper screen.

Directions

1. Cut two pieces of waxed paper the same length.
2. Arrange the selected materials on one sheet of waxed paper.
3. Place the second sheet of waxed paper on top.
4. Use a cool iron to melt the papers together.
5. Fold and staple construction paper strips over each end of the paper. Hang with yarn.

Materials

- Waxed paper
- Construction paper
- Stapler
- Scissors
- Yarn
- Iron
- Assorted materials such as: gold paper, scraps of tissue paper torn into bamboo shapes, glitter, pictures of trees and animals cut from magazines

JAPANESE MEAL

Historical Aid

Most Japanese food is cooked on a small grill called a *hibachi,* by broiling, steaming, simmering or frying. The basic menu consists of soup and three dishes, each cooked by a different method, followed by rice and pickles. Dessert, if it is served, is usually artistically cut fresh fruit.

When the table is set, it is the "rule" that no dish within one place setting match any other. The meal is laid out on low tables about the height of a coffee table and diners sit on low cushions. At each place there is a bamboo basket that holds a steaming towel to wipe face and hands.

Project

Have a tasting feast! Use the recipes on the following pages to prepare an authentic Japanese meal that includes soup, rice, pickles and three side dishes, each prepared by a different method. Serve fresh fruit along with the meal.

After the meal has been eaten, complete the Meal Comparison chart on page 27.

Materials

- Ingredients for recipes on following pages
- Electric skillets
- Cutting boards
- Knives and cooking utensils
- Pot holders
- Bowls, plates and chopsticks
- Garnishes, such as thin carrots slices cut with a tiny scalloped cutter or fresh parsley
- Tablecloth
- Lanterns or flowers
- Folding table
- Boxes
- Pillows

Directions

1. On a long table, set out cutting boards and let the students help cut the fruit and vegetables for the recipes you have chosen.

2. While the food is cooking, set the table with a tablecloth and some paper lanterns (see page 44) or fresh flowers. If your students want a chance to eat truly Japanese style, use folding tables with the legs closed and placed on sturdy boxes for a table the right height. Be sure to sit on pillows on the floor.

3. If serving "buffet style", instruct the diners to use the thick end of the chopsticks to pick up food from the serving dish, or provide serving chopsticks.

Tamago Suimono (egg soup)

Tamago Suimono

6 cups (1419.6 ml) *dashi*
  (substitute clear chicken broth)
1 tablespoon (14.8 ml) *shoyu*
  (soy sauce)
3 eggs
1 stalk celery, minced into tiny
  pieces

Directions: Bring chicken broth and soy sauce to a boil. While the broth is heating, beat the eggs well. After the broth comes to a boil, turn off the heat and pour in the eggs in a thin stream stirring the soup constantly. The eggs will set.

To Serve: Divide into small bowls and sprinkle on a little minced celery. Hold the soup bowl in your right hand and rest it in the palm of your left hand. Sip from the bowl as if it were a cup. It is customary to make a slurping noise!

Gohan (rice)

Directions: Rinse rice in cold water and drain. Place in pot with four cups water and bring to a rolling boil. Continue boiling for one minute. Cover, reduce heat and simmer without stirring or peeking for 20 minutes. This makes a fluffy, slightly sticky rice that is easy to pick up with chopsticks.

To Serve: Serve in pretty bowls, ungarnished.

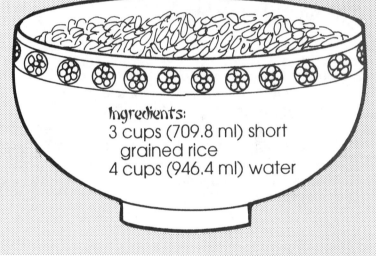

Ingredients:
3 cups (709.8 ml) short
  grained rice
4 cups (946.4 ml) water

Tsukemono (pickles)

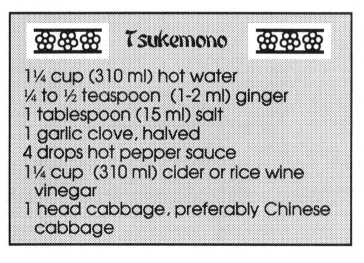

Tsukemono

1¼ cup (310 ml) hot water
¼ to ½ teaspoon (1-2 ml) ginger
1 tablespoon (15 ml) salt
1 garlic clove, halved
4 drops hot pepper sauce
1¼ cup (310 ml) cider or rice wine
  vinegar
1 head cabbage, preferably Chinese
  cabbage

Directions: In a large bowl, dissolve salt and ginger in hot water. Allow to cool. Meanwhile, cut cabbage into small pieces. Add to bowl along with remaining ingredients. Mix well. Pack into a quart-sized jar and cover tightly. Allow to stand at room temperature for one day. The pickles are then ready to serve. Refrigerate any leftovers.

Umani (meatballs)

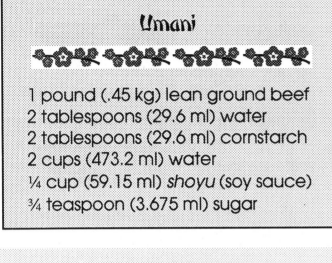

Umani

1 pound (.45 kg) lean ground beef
2 tablespoons (29.6 ml) water
2 tablespoons (29.6 ml) cornstarch
2 cups (473.2 ml) water
¼ cup (59.15 ml) *shoyu* (soy sauce)
¾ teaspoon (3.675 ml) sugar

Directions: Mix meat, two tablespoons water and cornstarch together. Form into small balls. Combine two cups water, soy sauce and sugar and bring to a boil. Reduce heat, add meatballs and simmer about 12 minutes.

To Serve: Place two meatballs in a bowl with a little broth. Garnish with a thin carrot slice cut into a flower, a tiny bunch of alfalfa sprouts or fresh parsely. Makes 40 small meatballs.

Steamed Vegetables

Directions: Cut carrots into long matchsticks. Place vegetables into steamer rack and place over boiling water. Steam until tender.

To Serve: Arrange a few vegetables on a dish. A little soy sauce may be used for dipping. Hold the sauce dish in your hand when using your chopsticks.

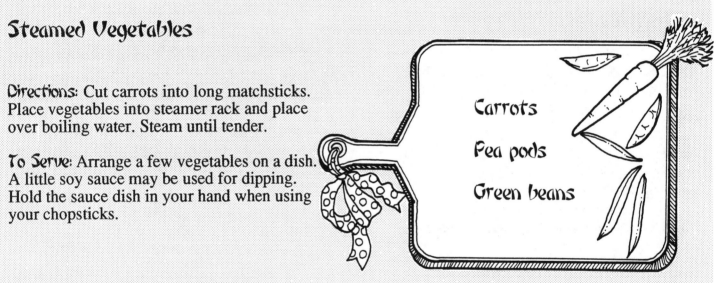

Carrots

Pea pods

Green beans

Kyuri-momi (cucumber salad)

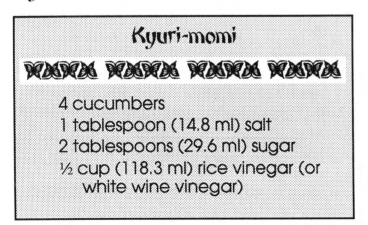

Kyuri-momi

4 cucumbers
1 tablespoon (14.8 ml) salt
2 tablespoons (29.6 ml) sugar
½ cup (118.3 ml) rice vinegar (or white wine vinegar)

Directions: Slice cucumber in half lengthwise. Scrape out the seeds. Cut into very thin slices. Sprinkle with salt and let set for 20 minutes. Rinse off salt in a colander under running water and let drain. Press gently to squeeze out water. Mix sugar and vinegar together. Pour over cucumbers.

To Serve: Mound a little salad in a bowl and garnish with a sprinkle of grated carrot. Makes 20 small servings.

Meal Comparison

☼ Japan ☼

Breakfast
Rice with a raw egg, beaten with soy sauce
and poured over the rice
Miso soup
Pickled vegetables
Salted plum
Tea

Lunch
Rice
Simmered vegetables
Fresh fruit
Fish
Tea

Dinner
Sashimi (raw fish)
Steamed custard made with
chicken and vegetables
Tempura (fried fish and shrimp)
Clear soup
Pickles
Rice
Tea

❦ My Diet ❦

Breakfast
_____
_____
_____
_____

Lunch
_____
_____
_____

Dinner
_____
_____
_____
_____

---

1. Fill in what you usually eat during the day.

2. How does your diet compare to what a Japanese person eats?

3. Which diet has more variety?

4. Which diet is more nutritious?

5. Which lunch is easier to take to school in a lunch sack?

6. Why do you think people in Japan eat so much seafood?

CHOPSTICKS

Historical Aid

Hashi, or chopsticks, are used to eat Japanese food. There is a proper way to use chopsticks. *Mayoi, sashi* and *yose*, which mean "dithering", "stabbing" and "drawing near" are considered bad manners. Please do not wave your chopsticks over the food, stab it or use your chopsticks to pull a serving dish to you!

Lift a dish off the table with one hand and use your hashi with the other. When eating a dish like *sashimi* (raw fish) use the hand not holding the hashi to hold the dish containing the sauce.

Project

Play a game that gives students a chance to practice using chopsticks by picking up a variety of items off a table.

Materials

- Chopsticks (available at most grocery stores)
- Different items of varying sizes for the students to practice picking up, such as:
  - ◆ cotton balls
  - ◆ dried beans
  - ◆ uncooked macaroni
  - ◆ pencil erasers
  - ◆ small wads of paper
  - ◆ rubber bands

Directions

1. Spread out the selected items on a long table.

2. Give each participant a set of chopsticks.

3. Give everyone a chance to practice holding and handling the chopsticks.

   - Instruct players to hold one chopstick like a pencil, slightly toward the thick end.

   - Next, slide the second chopstick between the thumb and second finger so it rests on the middle finger.

   - Hold the lower chopstick steady, and practice moving the upper chopstick only.

4. Choose four players for each game. On the shout of "*hashi*" the game begins!

5. The first player to pick up one of each item is the winner!

FANS

Historical Aid

The folding fan was invented in Japan nearly 1,300 years ago. Some historians speculate that the inventor of the first folding fan was inspired by a bat folding its wings.

Japanese fans are often painted in beautiful, bright colors. They are still used today in traditional dance and theater productions.

Project

Make a Japanese paper fan.

Directions

1. If using plain paper, decorate with markers, watercolors or crayons.

2. Fold paper widthwise into pleats approximately ¾ inch (1.905 cm) wide.

3. Cut tagboard into strips the same length and width as the folded fan. Glue these strips to the outside pleats and fasten closed with a rubber band until dry.

4. Tape around the bottom several times to make the handle. Remove rubber band and unfold.

Materials

- Wrapping paper from a roll and cut to 30" X 8" (76.2 cm X 20.32 cm) *or* three sheets of white or colored construction paper taped together lengthwise

- Crayons, markers or watercolors

- Tape

- Rubber bands

- Glue

- Tagboard

- Scissors

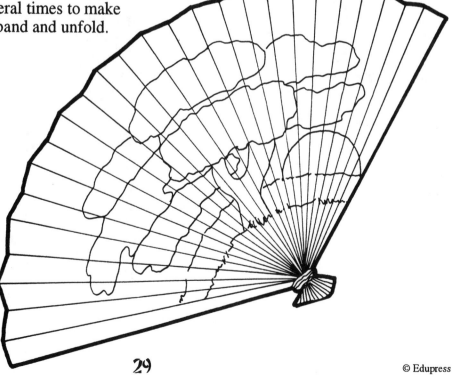

NOH THEATER

Historical Aid

When attending a *Noh* theater performance, the audience gets a chance to use their imagination! In this traditional performing art, which has been unchanged for 600 years, the stage is nearly bare and the only backdrop is a painted pine tree. The players move in stylized dance-like motions that are often remote from realistic movements. Three percussion instruments, a flute and chanting accompany the actors during performances that are still popular today.

Masks and costumes are an essential part of Noh. Many costumes and masks in use today are over 200 years old!

Project

Make a traditional Noh style mask.

Directions

1. Round off the edges of the tagboard pieces.

2. Pencil in the outlines of the facial features keeping in mind that Noh masks are used to display emotions.

3. Cut out the eye openings and a flap for the nose. Bend the nose flap forward.

4. Color brightly using crayons, paint or markers.

5. Use black construction paper to make hair. Tape or glue the hair to the back of the mask.

6. Tape two yarn pieces on the back of the mask near the eye holes for ties.

Materials

• Tagboard cut into pieces 9" X 13" (22.86 cm X 33.02 cm)

• Pencils

• Crayons, tempera paints or markers

• Black construction paper

• Scissors

• Yarn cut into 12 inch (30.48 cm) pieces

• Tape and/or glue

MUSIC

Historical Aid

Traditional music of Japan is performed by small ensembles composed of singers, woodwinds, stringed instruments and percussion instruments, such as drums and gongs. These groups are an integral part of the performing arts as they not only set the scene, but also convey the mood.

Taiko are drums that can range in size from hand held to seven feet tall and 700 pounds! A taiko may even be used to create effects such as falling snow when accompanied by tiny bits of paper falling from the top of the stage.

Project

Make a taiko drum and practice making music based on the sounds of nature.

Materials

• Construction paper

• Empty oatmeal boxes with lids

• Glue

• Scissors

• Crayons or markers

Directions

1. Decorate the construction paper with crayons or markers and glue it around the oatmeal box.

2. Practice making your music sound like rain. Start by lightly tapping with one finger then add more and more "raindrops" until you have a downpour. What other nature music can you think of?

3. Add other percussion instruments to your ensemble.

GLUE

NEW YEAR'S FESTIVAL

Historical Aid

New Year's Day is a very special celebration in Japan. The entire family cleans the house and yard before enjoying three days of celebration that begin January 1st. A simple meal of noodles is served on *O-misoka,* New Year's Eve. On *Gantan,* New Year's Day, everyone dresses in new clothes. A game similar to badminton may be played. Traditionally, this game of *hago asobi* was played only by girls. The *hago,* or shuttlecock, was made from feathers and soap-berry tree seeds and the wooden paddles were decorated with pictures of famous actors.

Project

Have the children help clean the classroom! Celebrate with a game of hago asobi.

Materials

- Cardboard
- Paint stirrers
- Magazines
- Scissors
- Small foam balls
- Feathers
- Glue
- Pattern, following

Directions

1. Reproduce and paste the pattern to the cardboard. Cut out the pattern shape.

2. Cut pictures from magazines and glue to the back of the paddle.

3. Glue the paint stirrer leaving a five-inch (13 cm) handle.

4. Stick two feathers into the foam ball to make a shuttlecock.

5. No net is necessary. Play in teams of two and see how long you can keep the hago in the air.

Hago Pattern

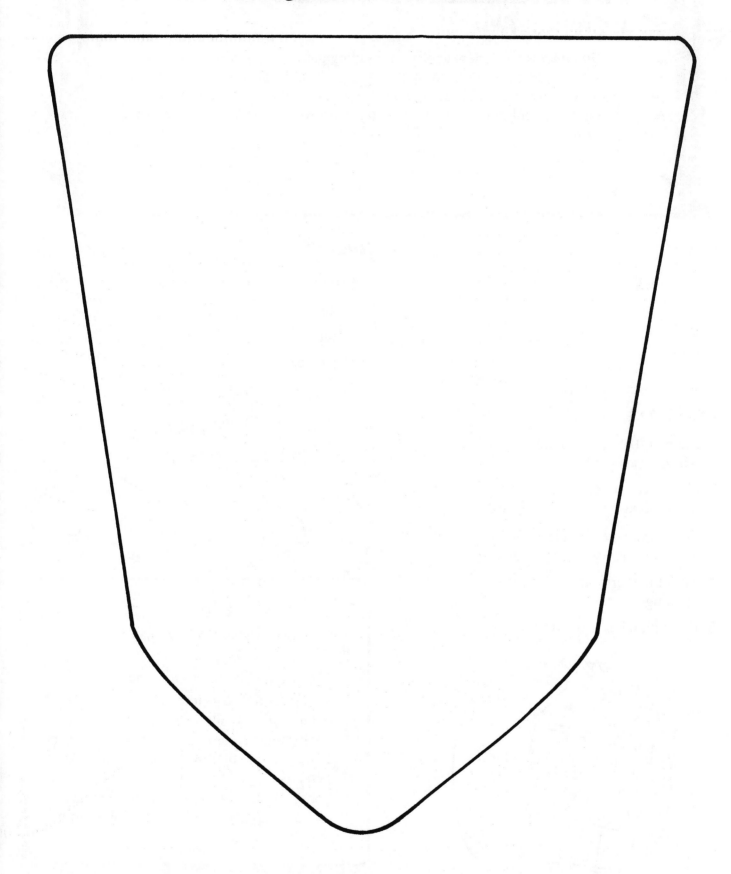

OTEDAMA

Historical Aid

Otedama is an ancient Japanese juggling game that is still played today. Bean bag type balls are used by the players. The purpose of the game is to see how many of the brightly colored balls can be kept in the air at once.

Japanese children fill their otedama with azukiu beans, but any dried beans will do.

Project

Make a set of otedama to juggle.

Materials

- Brightly colored fabric
- Needles
- Thread
- Dried beans
- Scissors

Directions

1. Cut 4" (10.16 cm) round circles from the fabric—two per ball.

2. Place two circles together with the printed sides facing.

3. Stitch around the circle ¼" (0.64 cm) from the edge leaving an opening at the top.

4. Turn the fabric right side out through the opening.

5. Fill with beans and stitch shut.

Otedama

1. Each player needs one otedama.
2. Players stand in a circle.
3. One person has all the otedama.
4. This person throws one ball at a time to another player, always the same player.
5. Each player in turn throws the ball he or she catches to another player, always the same person.
6. Soon, all the balls are in the air! This looks like a complicated maneuver, but is simple and fun.

BOYS' DAY

Historical Aid

Boys' Day shares May 5th with various kite festivals. Some families fly one *koi nobori*, or climbing carp streamer, for each boy in the family. Koi, or carp, are a symbol of courage and longevity. Climbing carp are carp that are going upstream. They are very strong and never give up.

In 1948, Japan adopted a new national holiday called *Kodomo No Hi* or Children's Day. It is celebrated on May 5th with ceremonies that bring together youth organizations and school representatives to honor all Japanese children.

Project

Make a *koi nobori*. These streamers can be hung from the ceiling to decorate the classroom.

Materials

- Light colored butcher paper 30" X 24" (76.2 cm X 60.96 cm)
- Pencil
- Colored markers or crayons
- Scissors
- Stapler
- Glue
- Strips of tagboard 1" X 12" (2.54 cm X 30.48 cm)
- Newspaper (optional)

Directions

1. Fold butcher paper in half lengthwise. Trace the carp design on one side making the folded edge the bottom of the fish. Cut out and decorate.

2. Staple or glue the top edge of the carp together being careful to keep the mouth and tail open. Lightly stuff with newspaper and staple the tail closed.

3. Staple the tagboard strip to the mouth to make a holder.

DOLLS' FESTIVAL

Historical Aid

On March 3rd, a Japanese girl might celebrate *Hina Matsuri*, or Dolls' Festival, by wearing a pretty kimono, displaying her special dolls and serving tea cakes and rice wine to her family and friends.

To display her dolls, a Japanese girl spreads a bright red cloth over a step-like structure with five to seven levels called a *hinadan*. She arranges her collection, usually consisting of a set of 15 porcelain and cloth dolls that might include an emperor and empress and their royal court. These beautiful dolls are symbolic ornaments, not toys.

Project

Plan a day for the students to share their own collections with their class.

Materials

- Red butcher paper (or a red tablecloth)
- One copy of the "My Collection" form, following, for each student

Directions

1. Cover a long table (or several desks pushed together) with red butcher paper or a red tablecloth. You may want to use books or boxes to make a second tier.

2. Give each student a copy of the "My Collection" form to complete.

3. Have the students arrange their collections and their "My Collection" form on this small version of a hinadan.

4. Arrange a time for the students to browse through the displays or have each student explain his collection aloud to the class.

My Collection

I have a collection of _____

I have been collecting since I was _____ years old.

My favorite thing in my collection is _____

It is my favorite because

_____

_____

I chose to collect these things because

_____

_____

I have_____ things in my collection.

This is what is the same for all the things in my collection.

_____

_____

This is what is different about the things in my collection:

_____

_____

The first item in my collection is

_____

_____

This is what came from the farthest away:

_____

KITES

Historical Aid

There are many legends about kites in Japanese lore as they have been flown there for centuries. One story tells of a warrior who made a large kite which he flew over the enemy's castle before going into battle. Another legend tells of a robber who used a kite to steal gold from the Golden Fish.

Different parts of Japan have kite festivals at various times throughout the year. Be careful you don't loose your kite on festival day. According to some legends, it will bring you bad luck. Kites are created in many shapes and designs—some look like octopi with long waving tentacles.

Project

Make a Japanese-style *ika-bata*, or cuttlefish kite.

Directions

Follow the step by step instructions on the following page to make a cuttlefish kite.

Materials

- One thin wooden stick, about one yard (one meter) long
- Butcher paper cut into a 25 inch (63.5 cm) square
- Glue
- Scissors
- Markers or crayons
- String
- Sandpaper

Cuttlefish Kite

1. With a sharp knife, score a line down the center length of the stick. Snap the stick in half over a table edge. Break one length at the 30" (76.2 cm) mark. Sand edges.

2. Use scissors to make two notches on the end of each slat. Cross the slats, make an X and lash the intersection **tightly** with string. To make the frame, connect the slats by running the string through the notches, making sure the string is pulled snug.

3. Decorate the paper using crayons or markers. Pictures of storks or tortoises are traditional, as are bands of red, light blue and white.

4. Lay the frame on the back of the paper, fold over the edges and glue.

5. Make a tail by cutting white butcher paper into 1" X 36" (2.54 cm X 91.44 cm) strips and gluing several to the bottom point of the kite. This tail is what makes the kite look like a cuttlefish.

6. Add string as illustrated. Kite string works best.

GAME OF TAG

Historical Aid

All around the world, children enjoy playing tag. The Japanese version is called "The Fisherman" and is a favorite recess time game along with dodgeball and volleyball!

Project

Play a game of "The Fisherman". This is an ideal game to play with a class on the playground.

Materials

- Chalk
- A playground or parking lot

Directions

1. Choose one player to be the fisherman. The rest of the players are the fish.

2. Using the chalk, draw a lake on the blacktop making the shore line very irregular. You want to have many "peninsulas".

3. The fish must stay in the "lake" and the fisherman must stay on the shore.

4. To play the game, the fisherman tries to catch the fish by running along the lake edge and tagging a fish. When the fisherman "catches" a fish, that player must leave the lake.

5. The last fish left in the lake becomes the next fisherman.

TEA CEREMONY

Historical Aid

Visiting a friend for tea in Japan traditionally means a ceremony that can last up to four hours! Before the ceremony begins, guests visit the garden and purify their hands in the outdoor fountain. They join their host in kneeling before an alcove that is decorated with a scroll and flowers (see page 8). It is quiet and peaceful and the precise steps taken to prepare and pour tea are designed not only to relax the guest, but also make them feel special. In fact, the host does not usually share in the refreshments unless invited to by the guests.

Project

Have a *chanoyu,* or tea ceremony, in your classroom. Divide the students into two groups and have them take turns pouring each other tea.

Directions

1. If possible, push the desks to one side of the room. Spread out the *tatamis* the children made from page 22 or use any floor mats.

2. You may wish to decorate your classroom with scrolls and lanterns that the students have made from page 44.

3. Great care goes into the arrangement of food on the plate, even for the simplest dish. Allow the server a chance to arrange the dish and cup on the tray, perhaps adding a flower or a paper fan.

4. Remember to fill the cup a little over half full to keep the top edge cool enough to pick up. It is customary to make a slurping noise as you sip the tea, especially if it is hot!

Materials

- Tea: green or herb
- Teapots, small paper plates and cups (preferably without handles)
- Serving trays *or* box lids lined with place mats
- *Tsujiura,* or Japanese fortune wafers
- Pillows to sit on
- Low tables or boxes

CLOTHING

Historical Aid

The traditional garment worn by both Japanese men and women is the *kimono*. It is a long garment with wide sleeves that wraps closed and ties snugly around the waist with a sash called an *obi*.

Traditional footwear includes high wooden clogs called *geta* and flat sandals called *gori*. These shoes have thongs that go between the first two toes. People never wear shoes inside a Japanese house. Shoes are left in the entryway and house slippers are worn indoors.

Project

Make a Japanese kimono and practice tying an obi.

Materials

- Extra large v-necked t-shirt
- Fabric scraps of assorted widths at least one yard (one meter) long
- Scissors
- Crayons
- Iron and brown paper bags (optional)
- Iron-on interfacing (optional)

Directions

1. Iron a 3" (7.62 cm) piece of fusible interfacing to the inside center front of the t-shirt, if desired, to keep the material from rolling.

2. Cut the t-shirt up the center front and on the dotted lines as shown.

3. Decorate with crayons. Optional: the crayon may be set by sandwiching the design between pieces of brown paper bag and pressing down with an iron. Set the iron on medium and do not move it back and forth across the design.

4. Use fabric strips for the ties.

5. TO TIE AN OBI: Wrap the kimono closed with the left side over the right. Boys tie a narrow sash in the front. Girls tie a wide sash into a flat bow in the back.

MARTIAL ARTS

Historical Aid

Japanese warriors began studying various methods of unarmed combat during the 12th century AD. These methods are still studied and practiced today in competitions. The word *karate* means "empty hand" and involves striking one's opponent with feet or hands. Competitors in a *judo* match attempt to throw their opponent and pin him down. *Kendo* is fencing with bamboo swords similar to those used by ancient samurai warriors. *Sumo* wrestling includes many ceremonial rituals. The wrestlers charge at each other in an attempt to push their opponent out of the ring.

Project

Practice exercising in the style of a sumo wrestler.

Materials

• Have students wear comfortable clothing

Directions

1. Exercise outdoors or push desks and chairs aside.

2. Form rows leaving plenty of space between students.

3. Have the students sway from side to side occasionally stamping their feet. Students yell, "YAH" as they stamp.

4. Next, have the "wrestlers" crouch down very low and be very still. As you signal, the students should take a giant frog leap as far as they can yelling, "YAH" as they jump.

5. Repeat as many times as you wish!

LANTERN FESTIVAL

Historical Aid

For three days in mid-July, Japanese Buddhists celebrate *Obon,* or the Festival of Lanterns. This festival is dedicated to the memory of friends and relatives who have died. On the first evening of the celebration, a lantern is lit and placed by the door as a symbol of welcome. During the next two days, families visit cemeteries, entertain guests and exchange gifts. On the evening of July 15th, the final day of the festival, families who live near the water gather for a special ceremony. Small paper lanterns are lit and set adrift on the water to guide the spirits of loved ones back to the other world.

Project

Make a variety of Japanese style lanterns.

Materials

- Black construction paper
- Scissors
- Colored tissue paper
- Light colored crayons
- Glue
- Construction paper in assorted colors
- Stapler

Directions

TISSUE PAPER LANTERNS

1. Fold black construction paper in half lengthwise.

2. Mark the design for the lantern on the folded paper using a light colored crayon.

3. Cut out the lantern.

4. Glue colored tissue paper pieces to the back of the lantern. Tape lanterns in a window. Sunlight passing through the tissue paper makes the lantern look lit!

CONSTRUCTION PAPER LANTERNS

1. Fold a piece of construction paper in half lengthwise.

2. Cut slits on the folded edge to within ½" (1.25 cm) of the open edge. Open and roll to form a lantern.

3. Staple top and bottom. Add a paper handle for hanging the lantern.

STAR FESTIVAL

Historical Aid

A favorite Japanese fairy tale tells the story of two heavenly stars who fall in love. Although they marry, they can be together only one day a year—on the seventh day of the seventh month. This happy day is celebrated in Japan with a Star Festival. Long bamboo poles are set up so they hang out over the streets. Colorful paper chains and streamers are fastened to the poles. Children decorate bamboo branches with paper figures. The day after the festival, these branches are set adrift in nearby streams to bring good luck to the celebrants.

Project

Make colorful streamers and paper chains to decorate a classroom as for a *Hoshi*, or Star Festival.

Materials

- Tagboard
- Various colors of crepe paper
- Stapler
- Scissors
- Glue or tape
- String
- Construction paper in assorted colors

Directions

1. Cut tagboard into a strip that will form the circle frame at the top of the streamer.

2. Glue or tape crepe paper strips to the tagboard strip.

3. Roll the tagboard into a circle and staple.

4. Attach string to each side of the cardboard circle to hang.

5. Make paper chains from various colored construction paper strips.

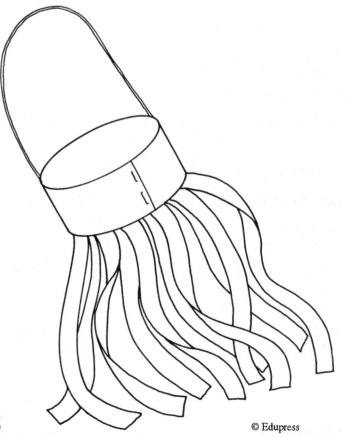

PUPPETS

Historical Aid

The puppets used in *Bunrako,* or puppet theater, vary in height from 3 to 4½ feet (.91 to 1.37 meters) and can weigh up to 40 pounds. These beautiful and elaborate costumed puppets require three men using levers and wires to manipulate their graceful movements. These men, although dressed in black, are visible to the audience. The puppets perform dramas based on Japanese history while narrators, accompanied by musicans, chant the story. Japanese families have been enjoying Bunrako since the late 16th century AD.

Project

Make a set of puppets and have a show.

Materials

- Puppet patterns, following pages
- Scissors
- Crayons or markers
- Paint stirrers (or craft sticks)
- Glue
- Tagboard

Directions

1. Reproduce the puppet patterns. Glue onto tagboard.

2. Color and cut out.

3. Glue the puppet onto the end of a paint stirrer or craft stick.

4. Have a puppet show. While one student reads a story from the literature list, other students can use their puppets to show the action. You may wish to have Japanese music playing in the background. Since the puppeteers are visible in Bunrako, simply cover a table or desk with a sheet and have the puppeteers wear black sweatshirts and stand behind the table.